Vibrant life on this planet is in peril. A human provoked peril that requires drastic human action.

If you do not believe this – or if you believe that the actions now being argued for will mitigate the worst consequences of a bio-calamity – then maybe this essay is not for you.

A Journey into A Future

Acknowledgements are made for the use of images and charts.

Shutterstock Images: Front and Rear covers; Plates III, VIII, XIII

Alami Images: Frontispiece

Adobe Images: Plates I, II, XI

Goya via British Museum: Plate IV
© The Trustees of The British Museum

Wellcome Images: Plate V

Tom Partridge (TOMP): Plate VI

Planet Centred Forum: Plate VII

Devolve! : Plate IX

Dignity in Dying: Plate X

British Museum: Plate XII
© The Trustees of The British Museum

F. Schmultzer/Austrian National Museum: Plate XIV

Elsevier: Plate XV

a Journey into a future

Part Three of the Values trilogy

Woody Wood

Devolve!

Leicester, England

Published by *Devolve!*
13 Biddulph Street
Leicester
England
LE2 1BH

A Journey / Woody Wood — 1st ed.

ISBN 978-0-9931126-2-1

Printed and bound by imprintdigital.com

A JOURNEY

into a Future

Paradise

To All Life on Planet Earth

... and to all Values Warriors defending Earth

THE INSIDE AND THE OUTSIDE OF LIFE

You have an inside and an outside.

On the *outside* i know you as an object, a creature. In this case a fellow human being on this planet that we share. On the *inside* you experience yourself as a bundle of sensations, feelings, memories, moods, hopes and fears, tensions and fulfilments.

As for you so for me. I am your object even as i experience myself.

Are we unique? Most unlikely. We can, we think, safely assume the same of other human beings around us.

Why stop there? Scaling down, there is no reason to assume that other creatures, even extending to plants and microbes, do not also experience themselves, even though they are objects to us. We might want to add the qualifier that entities with less complex structures experience themselves in a more rudimentary way.

We need not even stop there. i have argued elsewhere that even a stone, apparently a static object, may self-experience its atomic vibrations and any stresses that it is under.

What about scaling up? Living in an extremely, perhaps pathologically, individualistic age we find it difficult to concede reality to groups: as organisms that are more – and more complex – than the sum of their parts. Yet both traditional peoples and those who have to work closely with nature are usually aware of this. Animal groups also have an outside – they can be described – and an inside: they can experience mood swings for example; they can also possess wisdom beyond that of any individual member.

Why stop there? Again i have speculated in previous essays[1] that our Universe, the most complicated dynamic entity that we presently know, has an outside – we observe some of it – and an inside: that it knows all, remembers all, suffers all, enjoys all.

This view may not be quite as maverick as it seems. Over one hundred years ago the pioneers of quantum theory moved our understanding of the Universe from a mechanical one of 'billiard ball' objects interacting according to fixed rules ... to a dynamic one of interacting fields governed by probabilities. An electron, for example, is both a particle and a wave. Schrodinger's famous cat could be alive and dead at the same time.

Other branches of enlightenment science have been much more resistant to these more fluid ideas. The mainstream of evolutionary biology, for example, has in a sense gone backwards from the open minded approach of Charles Darwin[2] towards the inheritance of characteristics.

For the Neo-Darwinists[3] the 'billiard ball' gene continues to be the only mechanism for passing information down the line. Even the Lamarckian view that learnt wisdom could be inherited has been regarded as heretical by many.

Even more shocking to the orthodox has been the approach of Rupert Sheldrake[4], arguing a background field able to guide the development of an organism by *resonance* with all previous occurrences, both of its own history and of other similar events. One example of this universal field theory for which evidence is claimed is that if a particular experiment is once conducted in a laboratory in Boston (say) it becomes easier to repeat the experiment in (say) Melbourne.

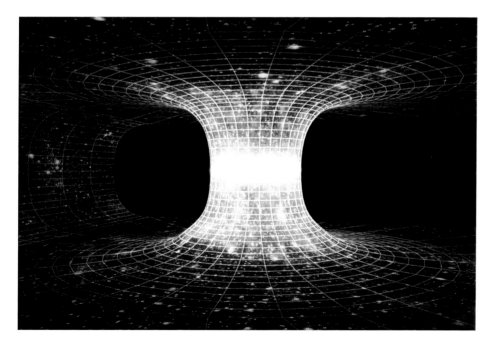

I.   *Quantum space*

THE GREAT DIVIDE

If there is one world, how come that science and religion perceive such different worlds today, seemingly unable to communicate? (It was not always so.) This gulf is troubling to many thoughtful people and throws up some bizarre contradictions. It was pointed out in an earlier essay that a scientist could be conducting an experiment in the enlightenment spirit of logical positivism on a Thursday and worshipping his God in church on a Sunday.

Could it be that modern science directs its attention to the outside of the world, the world as object, while the spiritual world view is engaging with the inside of the world, the world as passion? [In recent years scientific investigation has probed deeper into brain structure and mental states. Impressive as these advances are they are still explorations on the outside of the Universe.]

Is there prospect for a wisdom that could encompass both sides of the Universe?

At this stage it is necessary to be critical of both approaches, both 'traditions'. Or rather, to recognise that in both cases we have composites, entanglements, of deep wisdom, deep attunement, and – as Nietzsche would put it – "all too human" fallibility.

In the case of science, whether in ancient Greece or in the modern enlightenment, the core value, the golden nugget, was and is *integrity*. Several observers and practitioners have recognised this. Sadly, in efforts both to formalise and defend the scientific method two devices have been brought to the fore. The first of these is to extol objectivity – "how it really is" – as against subjectivity, the viewpoint of human beings with all their biases. The second is to claim that the scientist is able to stand outside the world, not a suffering part of it, and from this privileged position their objectivity is justified.

On the other side of the divide, spiritual/religious wisdom was and is rooted in *enchanted awe* with our world, combined with a sense of vulnerability before powerful forces. Alas the religious traditions gradually committed to written records and made 'holy' were in practice a combination of tapping into this deep wisdom, this empathy with nature and the cosmos, plus the 'all too human' cultural prejudices of their times – compounded by the desires of the newly emerging priest classes to consolidate their positions.

So in both cases, both approaches to the world, there are combinations of valid and invalid foundations. Recognising these compromises, these alloys of majesty and dross – taken together with the primary insight that our Universe, like us, has an observable outside and a suffering inside – could lay the foundations for a broader wisdom.

Julian Jaynes, in his neglected work *The Origin of Consciousness in The Breakdown of The Bicameral Mind*[5] charts the gradual loss of our ability to 'communicate with the gods'. He makes the point that the most effective communicators of the wisdom of the Oracle in ancient Greece – which continued to be respected for a thousand years – were uneducated country girls. Reason can be the enemy of wisdom.

Now we need to balance that provocative statement against the very real achievements of reason-led enlightenment science. Reason has proved a very powerful tool. Like all tools – say a hammer or a screwdriver – it is very useful for some purposes and unhelpful or even dangerous for others. The prospect of nuclear destruction is a fateful example.

A cardinal error of the enlightenment was in raising reason to the status of a god – perhaps because it thought it had abolished the old gods?

I dare to speculate that an intent of our Universe in evolving consciousness on certain planets has been to be able to contemplate itself from the outside, so to speak. Certainly cheeky and arrogant to even attempt to second guess the purposes of our greater world. Sorry.

II. Talking with God

III. *Enchantment*

THREATS TO OUR PLANET

Coming down to earth (sic) the threats to our own planet and the escalating tragedies for life on it are on the minds of some of us.

In physical terms the facts are already known to those who want to know them. Seven plus billion humans consuming already the greater part of the world's biomass, devouring its non-renewable resources as if there was no tomorrow (which might just be true), choking the planet with wastes and pollution, driving other species to the edge of extinction and beyond, playing with dangerous technologies like the sorcerer's apprentice...

To put this in context, nothing lasts for ever. It is reckoned that in about six hundred million years, as our sun starts to run out of hydrogen, it will expand to swallow the earth. That is a long way ahead.

On this timescale, with good stewardship by any wise species in partnership with Gaia, we could look forward to many more years of life revelling in itself. Again on this timescale the loss of one species – humanity – would not be such a tragedy. Certainly on a vote of the millions of now threatened species it (we) might be the top choice for an early exit.

Needless to say most humans would be rather sad about that. This gives some of us an incentive to use what wisdom we have to pursue that partnership with nature; that respect for Gaia, mentioned above. This could – will – involve some hard choices. To quote from the mission statement of Planet Centred Forum[6]: "If immediate human interests clash with ecosystem interests then the latter must be given priority".

Given that current human interests and priorities are light years away from such wisdom, maybe a place to start is a review of the human social structures and values that have paved the road of our journey into the present.

The most obvious change in human evolution has been increasing control over nature. The development of tools and weapons, mastery of fire, forethought and socially co-ordinated activities gradually elevated some pre-human and human groups from a precarious existence on the edge of survival to relatively assured ecological niches. From the perspective of other large mammals human bands were now to be feared.

Alongside these material developments, perhaps due to increased mental and social capacities, came increased awareness and self-awareness. Different relationships to the natural world, different attitudes, different *values* were now possible.

THE VALUES ISSUE

Assumptions about the world have always provided the framework for values (see appendix C). One trajectory was continued awe and respect for the still mighty natural world around them. It is recorded that some native peoples will say a prayer to the spirit of a tree before cutting it down to make their hut. Humility is still central to some spiritual traditions. In others this awe has been transferred from nature to a being, a force, above nature, leading to what has been called the de-sacralisation of the world.

This was the other path: a new confidence, even arrogance, in our human powers. One might surmise that this would more easily arise among elite groups within larger post-agriculture societies less directly dependent on the outcome of the harvest. As the story moves forward from ancient towards pre-modern times this narrative would be reinforced by increasing ability to understand and manipulate nature, whether in agriculture or manufactures.

Now in the Social Story of *Values for Our Time*[7] it was argued that most creatures are either collective or mainly solitary in their natures, whereas humans are among the few that exist on what was called the creative interface between collectivity and autonomy, with massive implications for social tensions and social discourse.

It was further argued that – perhaps starting with the nominalist philosophers in the middle ages (or were they just responding to changing social realities?) – the social pendulum was swinging towards individualism. The age of alienation was beginning. [The original meaning of

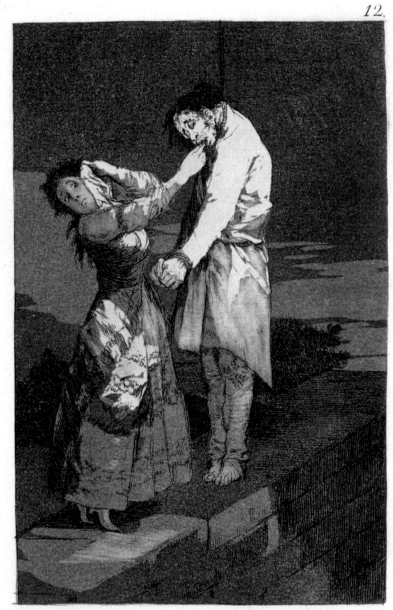

A caza de dientes.

IV. The alienation of feelings from actions

alienation was to sell, or alienate, a piece of traditional land. Thus the native chief in the newly occupied Americas who asked: "how can anyone own the land?"]

Alienation became a central focus of radical social philosophy. A classic example was *The Alienation of Modern Man* by Fritz Pappenheim[8], drawing on the insights of Marx and Tönnies.

The gradual loss of community to cosmopolitan individualism has been one of the foundations of *modernity*, defined by Dr Patrick Curry[9] as an unholy alliance of Techno Science, Neoliberal Capitalism and The State. Modernity, he argues, stands in contrast to human *enchantment* with the world: recognised earlier as a fundamental value in social communities.[10]

Lest we consider that all is already lost, another feature observed in both human individuals and social groups is their tendency to 'flip' from one mode of behaviour to another in response to certain triggers. Some of these modes are described in *Values for Our Time*. What provokes these mode flips in their social contexts is a proper subject for further exploration.

Where such rapid attitude shifts relate to human relations with, values towards, the natural world – as explored above – the task facing us becomes clear.

But who is 'us'? A challenging suggestion will be put forward later. In the meantime the relatively small numbers of pioneers both trying to live out and argue for planet centred values have been defined elsewhere[11] as *values warriors*. Are you some of them?

ALL THE OTHERS

To remind ourselves of the scale of the task let us consider the communities and the individuals who do not seem to share our anxieties for an endangered planet.

World-wide there are teeming millions whose first concern is sheer survival – a situation driven, directly and indirectly, by global consumption and population density. This in turn is driven partly by patriarchal cultures denying women control of their bodies and partly by the demands of the first world, in collusion with their own elites, for their food and commodities. These forces destroy natural communities as they are thrown off their land to make way for cash crops. [I witnessed this personally in Ghana where cash exports included not only cocoa but aluminium smelted from bauxite by electricity from the Volta dam (which flooded so much fertile land).]

Put yourself in their situation. Could you be blamed for supplementing your limited diet with bush meat, even though that is driving many animal species to extinction?

More generally there are millions, including in the first world, who simply do not think about the issue. This is partly because they are focussing on their own problems: families, including older relatives and children; jobs; housing; etc ... and partly because the connections have never been made clear to them. Most of us today are city dwellers (the population of Mexico City, for example, is 25 million and rising) and we are increasingly remote from nature. Here is an example of where bonded communities, including focussed sub‑groups, have more scope to consider the wider issues than struggling single families. [Appendix B]

Next of course there are the vested interests, driven by the bottom line of their giant corporations and often powerful enough to buy governments and media outlets. So much has been written about this that it hardly needs elaboration here.

Then there are the deniers, influential out of proportion to their numbers, whose message resonates with those who do not wish to hear bad news or to be challenged; plus all those who have learnt to be suspicious of experts and 'official' pronouncements. Included in this group, sadly, are socially concerned people who do not want to hear any facts that could pose difficulties for their social justice agenda. Unlike in the sixties and seventies when the issue of population was openly discussed, just to mention the word population in some Green Party and left wing circles today is to be considered fascist!

V. T. R. Malthus

The continued visceral hostility to Thomas Malthus[12] after more than two hundred years is a classic example. Now Malthus can certainly be criticised for many things, including his objection (on religious grounds) to contraception and his belief that the poor laws in England would encourage families to have more children than they could provide for. Yet the statement that he is so reviled for is simply pointing out that population – in the long run – has to stay in balance with food supply: that there are limits to what we can extract from the earth. (He was not of course aware of other constraints such as pollution.) This directly challenges our need to believe in an 'ever upwards' future.

Mention could be made here of Murray Bookchin who frequently crossed swords with deep green or planet centred pioneers. His classic work *The Ecology of Freedom*[13] was not strictly about ecology at all but rather a powerfully argued case for human emancipation and social justice across the planet, arguing (not unreasonably) that the defeat of the exploiters could make some other problems less intractable. In noting that Bookchin was intensely human centred mention should be made of an insight with massive implications for both philosophy and our view of the future in general. This was that humans were not just another animal species but – in their mental, psychological and social complexity – represented a leap in evolution as great as that between non-life and life on this planet. (The implications of this insight from Bookchin require serious consideration.)

The next group of dissenters may be called the 'blame the baddies' contingent: our plight is simply the result of capitalism or neo-colonialism. Now there is some truth in this (see above). The problem is that it exonerates most of us for our complicity in this system: whether our desire for cheap imports to feed our first world consumption or our need for good returns for our pension funds investments.

Lastly, we should mention the realists/fatalists. "Our world is doomed anyway so we might as well eat, drink and be merry."

SOME RESPONSES

Among those who do recognise a real problem and accept that we should attempt to do something about it (ruling out coercive or eugenicist solutions) there are a number of favoured actions. Across all of these there is a tension between those who feel that *only* governments can tackle such momentous issues (the Fabian fallacy); that *our* only role is simply to lobby them to do so … as against the understanding that *we* need to take responsibility, to organise and act out our convictions.

The above is not meant to imply that 'democratic' governments are always incapable of bold actions – rather that we need to recognise the powerful and conflicting lobby pressures that they are subject to. Beyond this, faith in existing nation states fails to recognise the different scales at which responses will be required [Appendix B]. Yet the core of the Fabian fallacy is that it both enables us to avoid the responsibility of acting ourselves and can undermine real 'bottom up' initiatives.

Coming back to the threat that we pose to the biosphere, the classic formula is $I = P \times C \times T$, where I is the total impact that we humans are having on the planet, P is the population making that impact, C is the rate at which we are consuming the planet's resources, T is the effect of the type of technologies that we are using.

The most common first response, because the least challenging, is faith in 'Green' technology: from the green revolution in agriculture to sources of renewable energy. While not denying the potential benefits, some of us would wish to argue that concentrating on such strategies as a total solution is dangerous on two counts.

First, we would draw attention to the hidden costs (such as rare minerals in solar panel manufacture) and unforeseen consequences (such as biodiversity loss in 'green revolution' crop yields). Perhaps more importantly, this search for 'painless' solutions can divert good people from facing up to more challenging issues.

POPULATION

Despite the hostility to even raising the subject referred to earlier, some of us who are committed to responding to the crisis for our biosphere do support

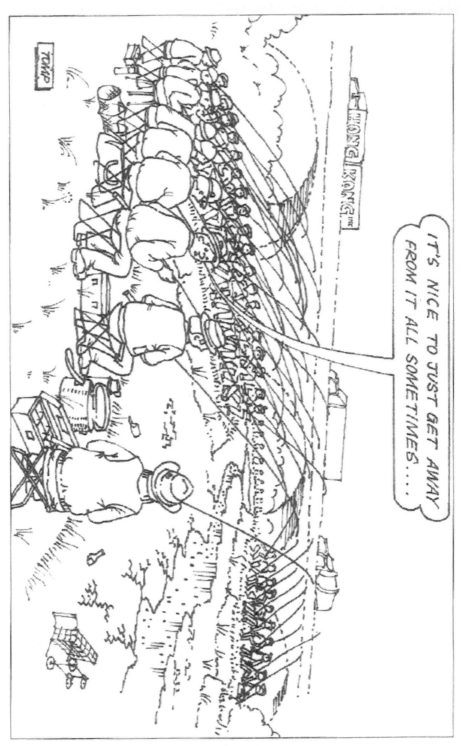

VI.

20

population reduction or at least some population growth reduction.

There are several downsides to this apparently desirable aim on the part of first world advocates. So what are the issues?

The least contentious strategy (among first world population radicals) is empowering women to have control over their own bodies, including access to reliable contraception.

Yet even this intention meets opposition from five directions. As one might expect many third world ruling elites see larger populations as a route to enhanced military power. Beyond this the Neoliberal commitment to continuous economic growth needs continually expanding markets which in turn requires ever more consumers. Then for 'traditional' cultural patriarchy the emancipation of women is directly challenging. There is also fierce opposition from the 'right to life' lobby who currently have a new champion. Last but not least many anti-imperial radicals across the world resent the neo-colonial implication of 'advice' from their first world cousins who have done little to put their own house in order – and they do have a point.

Notwithstanding all these factors, most of us would want to argue that reductions in birth rates that also enable some women to lead less desperate lives can be considered as win-win events. A requirement going forward is not just engagement with charities and others working on the ground to provide education and services but respectful partnerships with activists and organisations responding to the complex challenges in their social and political contexts.

Nearer to home, the population of England (in particular) is once again increasing at a rate that is unsustainable in the medium term, never mind the long term. Apart from rising social stresses and the impacts on resources here, including schools, health and care services, the consumption of foodstuffs and other crops imported from third world zones is distorting the economies of those areas.

CONSUMPTION

This leads us to the other element in the I=PCT equation: consumption. Now consumption is caused by consumers. The questions are: how many?... how much?... and for how long?

For most of evolutionary history animal behaviour (including human and pre-human behaviour) was regulated by the "law of least effort". With few exceptions animals only hunted when they were hungry. For our ancestors life was sometimes a struggle to survive. At other times there was just enough – for there was little incentive or means to hoard. Agriculture was to change all that.

POPULATION, CONSUMPTION and LONGEVITY - Visual Representations (not to scale)

Actual World Population Numbers

(source: World Population Clock)

First World Population : 1 Billion People

Rest of World Population
6.4 Billion People

World Equivalent Population Numbers

Taking account of consumption

Fraction of these beyond Seventy Years
2 Billion People Equivalent

First World Population
12 Billion People Equivalent
(source: Physics fact book money)

Rest of World Population
6.4 Billion People Equivalent

VII.

One does not need to endorse the whole Marxist narrative to honour some of the great insights and concepts of Karl Marx. One such was *surplus value*. Once any situation arose where human labour could produce more than the bare necessities needed for continued survival then this surplus value could accrue to the community – or to elements within the society able to appropriate and control it.

With the birth of agriculture and mass stratified societies these conditions were fulfilled. It was now possible to control serfs or keep slaves. As a toiler in the fields it was no longer feasible to obey your own law of least effort. There were great warehouses to fill ... and from this store of wealth the warrior and the priest castes could command the labour to build pyramids and temples; forts and navies.

This principle of expropriation of surplus continued through history. In England the post-conquest Doomsday Book of 1087 was a survey to see how much surplus value could be extracted as taxes from the conquered people. The Victorian mill owners whom Marx was able to study at first hand raised surplus value extraction to a fine art. Today most of us are familiar with the mantra that 1% of the people control 99% of the wealth. The surplus value of our labours is certainly not in our pockets despite our relative historical affluence.

In the last few generations a new factor has entered the equation. The traditional exploitation model aimed to leave the toilers with just enough to maintain themselves. Yet as the productivity of the economic system continued to advance the problem of markets – customers – for the products came to the fore. The genius of Henry Ford was to lower the price of his Model T just enough that blue collar workers could aspire to buy one. For the first time in history *they* needed *us* as consumers and not just as producers.

At a stroke (strictly it was more gradual than that) we became complicit in the system of ever expanding production, consumption, profit and waste. At first the 'pent up demand' (economist's phrase) for a better life was very real. In the later stages enormous and growing effort is being devoted to persuading us that we need to consume more and more of just about everything – and it mostly works.

Putting this in the context of our impact on the planet, some recent calculations [see plate 7 and appendix A] indicate that typical first world consumption is *twelve times* consumption in the rest of the world, where most people still live. This can be expressed by a useful concept: the *equivalent population* of the first world, taking the number of people in the rest of the world as a point of reference. This shows that, due to our massive consumption, our total impact is about twice that of the rest of the world. We are about one billion people yet act like twelve billion. Scary.

Trouble is that most of us in 'advanced' economies don't see ourselves as over-consumers. We are not the super-rich are we? For many of us our incomes barely seem to keep up with our spending. Flying to holidays in the sun feels like a near necessity to make the work grind bearable. A new gadget like an iPhone appears and in no time our lifestyles have grown into them. And then there is the housing issue: oh gosh the housing!

CONSUMPTION, INCOME AND WEALTH

Going into this a bit deeper reveals a number of difficult issues and ethical dilemmas. For a start, most of us are well aware that wealth is not the not the same thing as income.

For most of the 'doing all right' a lot of wealth today is stored in housing; often their own but in some cases second homes bought for extra income. On the other hand there are those with quite good incomes who are not able to get on the housing ladder in affluent parts of the country. They often pay a double whammy of rents and commuting fares without gaining wealth. Those with new mortgages also pay out a lot of their income to others but in theory are gaining bricks as wealth. (In fact the early years of mortgage repayments are mostly interest.)

Now wealth can offer security and power yet it is not itself consumption. Ebenezer Scrooge in the Charles Dickens novel would have had very low consumption! It is the relatively poor who are likely to spend almost all of their personal incomes on things and services – they are the 'best' consumers.

Taking a broader view, those of us living in more affluent countries can divide our total consumption into three categories. First, social infrastructure over which we have very little direct control. This includes everything from roads to rubbish collection plus health and social services, education of children and so on. Second, being housed plus basic bills plus relative necessities: where we have control in theory but not much in practice. Third, more general spending where we have more scope to make choices on both the quantity and nature of our consuming.

Another quote from Dickens (Mr Pickwick): "Neither a borrower nor a lender be". Well, that advice is certainly not heeded today. Lenders do not know when to stop in their greed for more and more profit from usury: the collapse of the so-called sub-prime housing market (risky lending cleverly packaged as sound bonds) almost took the world economy down in 2008. Borrowers do not know when to stop either in their determination to consume all the 'must have' good things that the market tempts them with. Pawnbrokers and other high street lenders step in to meet that demand at annual rates of interest of typically 240%.

We, as planet centred radicals, may do what we can to challenge ourselves, and encourage others, to limit consumption in those areas where we do have some choice.

In some cases less absolute, more pragmatic stances might actually achieve more. An example would be around flying. We have argued elsewhere that "fly only once a year" could be a more credible challenge than "do not fly". The nature of our consumption may also matter. Especially with edible or wearable items, issues such as food miles, land impoverishment, local economies, organic and fair trade choices, wild life impacts etc could all be factors in our decisions.

A major dilemma in the economies that we are locked into is that our consumption creates the jobs of others. In the extreme, the livelihoods of families in the nuclear weapons related industries depend on 'our' decision not to risk unilateral nuclear disarmament...

BACK TO POPULATION

It is clear that all our attempts in the first world to limit our consumption in those areas where we do have some measure of choice are fraught with dilemmas and inevitable compromises. The only sure way to limit our twelve-fold consumption is *not to be here*. What?

VIII. Population Generations

It was noted earlier that the three questions relating to total consumption were: How Many (consumers)? How much (consumption per head)? plus How Long (to consume for)?

We know that how many is presently too many. Others[14] have estimated that a human population for long term eco-stability and gradual recovery of the biosphere, including species diversity, might be half a billion – still many times more than other great apes.

We have just looked at the issues and difficulties around both social and personal consumption, especially in the 'rich North'.

Now the classical figure for a proper human lifespan is "three score years and ten". Most people never reached that number, nor do they today. (Shakespeare died at fifty though he managed to pack quite a lot in.) Seen in this context the lifespans that many of us aspire to in the first world are a historical and geographical abnormality. They have been made possible by medical and infrastructure advances and by massive consumption of resources dedicated to extending our lives and dealing with the consequences of chronic health conditions. Refer to appendix D.

These developments have taken place in the context of changing social values. In previous times it was accepted that life was hard and transient; that suicide (for example)

When there is no community:-

Each individual looks to their own interest

'The other' becomes an object, perhaps a threat

Leaders become a class for their own advantage

The devil takes the hindmost

Crime and poverty flourish

Crime is legalized (for some) as property and usury

IX.

31

was a noble and responsible act of judgement. Then we became God's property (later the State's property): exiting life became shameful; assisting a person to die – even a loved one in appalling terminal pain and indignity – remains a major crime in many parts of the world. (This is starting to change: California and Canada are among legislatures where assisted dying is becoming approved under strict safeguards.)

Fairly recently the rise of liberal morality exemplified by John Stuart Mill has exalted the human individual over the social community. (Two hundred years earlier John Donne had reminded us that "no man is an island".) The mantra "every human life is precious", apart from being homocentric (what about other lives?) and hypocritical (e.g. civilian deaths in 'just' wars) denies the complex tensions that humanity has always wrestled with and which may now overwhelm us. The liberal notion of protecting individual human lives is applied selectively in practice. Some humans in wealthier communities are both the leading advocates and the main beneficiaries. Such attitudes may now obstruct a clear view of those actions that offer the best hope for all life.

Perhaps influenced by modern liberal values most of those concerned about the impact of human numbers advocate slowing the birth rate as the most humane response to overpopulation. In fact this is already happening in some parts of the world for a variety of reasons. A consequence of this change is the changing ratio

X. *Lobbying Westminster*

of young to old. Ageing populations have now become a serious issue for many societies and one that is certainly ringing alarm bells.

I want to argue now a more fundamental objection. Across almost all of nature the existential imperative has been, and is, to bring forth and nurture the young. (The case for supporting the limitation of *unwanted* third world births through education and contraception has been made.) So to devote precious resources to un-naturally extending the lives of those of us who have already had our share of living time, probably enjoyed our best years, plus (in many cases) consumed far more than our share of the planet's resources … *is in conflict with life's imperative.*

How should values warriors respond? Each of us can allow ourselves to be open to the possibility of an exit to make room for the future – for our own offspring down the line, for the descendants of other humans, most of all for all the life forms now being pushed to the edge of extinction and beyond.

EXIT IS NOT EASY

The point was made earlier that even those in extreme terminal pain with an appalling quality of life are prevented from being enabled to die in many – though not all – legislatures across the world at this time. (In the state of Oregon, which has permitted assisted termination for some years now, the fears of those who formerly opposed the change as a 'slippery slope' have proved to be unfounded.)

The London based organisation Dignity in Dying[15] exists both to support those (and their partners/carers) in this tragic situation and to campaign for a change in the law.

****

The starting point for values warriors is very different. By definition values warriors love life, say 'yes' to life, are concerned for all life.

They are aware of the growing threat to the biosphere from human population and consumption plus the part that first world longevity contributes to such pressures.

Balancing their own part in this against the contribution that they hope to be making by raising general awareness, values warriors *may* decide that personal exit is the most pro-life decision that they can make.

The obstacles are formidable... Perhaps the first challenge is the 'stay alive at all costs' (and regardless of consequences) culture so dominant today. This can extend to well-meaning friends and allies, even those who profess deep green or ecocentric convictions.

XI. *Too many people?*

Now the requirement for achieving global impact, as and when a widespread mode flip is triggered (see previous reference to the Social Story of *Values for Our Time*) is that exit decisions be understood as pro-life decisions, taken for the greater good. At present they are at risk of being classed as suicides (by both coroners and the general public).

Suicide, for whatever reason, is the supreme act of saying 'no' to life: "I do not want this vale of tears". It cannot be stated too clearly that values warriors – like most people – love life, are in love with life, yet can respond to social imperatives. The fireman who enters a burning building in an attempt to save lives; the onlooker who plunges into a stormy sea in an (often vain) attempt to rescue another human being in difficulties; plus of course the soldier on the battlefield … would be most insulted to be called suicides. Here is another mountain to climb.

The third challenge is a practical one. Most authorities have gone out of their way to ban or make unavailable the tools, whether barbiturates or other, that would enable a safe, certain and peaceful exit. There are choices such as travelling abroad or illegally importing internet purchases but again these roads are open to a few with the means and determination to act rather than being democratically available – a citizen's right.

Lastly and perhaps most intimidating there are the severe penalties (in some regimes) on doctors, friends and loved ones deemed to have assisted. Advice on these latter issues may be obtained from Exit International[16].

As mentioned earlier, an alternative in the first world may be extremely frugal consumption – an exit from consumption if you like. It was pointed out just how difficult this was to achieve since much of this was collective infrastructure consumption and/or the allocation of resources to prolonging life beyond our sell by dates.

Now notwithstanding the caution expressed earlier regarding the limited scope that national states have to act, as the desperate situation for both human and non-human life on the planet becomes clearer states might one day be challenged to limit artificially extended longevity: at the same time easing the spiralling fiscal burden of prolonging life at (literally) all costs and also addressing the distortion of the population age spectrum.

THE DISCONNECT

There appears to be a disconnect, especially among greens and other radicals, between the general stance "urgent action is needed to save our planet" and personal commitments that could make a small but perhaps incremental difference going forward. It seems that *someone else* has to do it, to be exhorted to do it.

Even in those areas where personal choices are possible the resistance to radical courses of action – say not flying or not being complicit in cattle culture – is simply staggering: or would be to a visiting Martian.

So are campaigning radicals really the best pathfinders?

As a result of many conversations with 'ordinary people' (i.e. not ecologically or socially concerned radicals) two stories have emerged.

First, they are not generally oblivious to the situation, in need of education, as is often supposed. It seems as if, deep in their collective wisdom, there is understanding that we have probably blown it. (This could relate to Rupert Sheldrake's thesis of fields that influence behaviour.)

Second, i found a widespread, though not perhaps universal, judgment that it was better to enjoy the fruits of modern living until we have to stop. Death was not the dominant issue for most it seemed: lack of amenity (say a car) was more critical.

Should say that most of these views were expressed by 'mature' people. Which leads on to the next sections.

A CHANGING WORLD

Traditionally the elders of the tribe were looked to as a store of wisdom and as the guardians of the values handed down. There is still truth in this. Certainly the experience that living brings can be a social asset. Yet wisdom is not only what you know but what you know that's wrong – or rather no longer appropriate to new times.

In a human world where social and technical change was relatively gradual the 'wisdom of the elders' mantra had some good justification. For recent generations and especially in recent decades these changes are so rapid that the core of social knowledge can be said to reside with the young – and what their elders assumed true is often no longer relevant to the future.

Another of the great insights of Karl Marx was the *time lag* between (in his language) the mode of production and the relations of production. In other words, between the balance of economic (plus informational) forces and the ordering of society that formerly reflected that balance. Marx argued that the build-up of tensions as this discrepancy grew would lead to major social upheavals. A classic example was the English Civil War (to Marxists the Bourgeois Revolution) between the traditional and originally land based aristocracy under the King and the rising power of the merchants and bankers (plus the new East Anglian land barons) represented by Parliament.

XII. Cult Goddess

Merlin Stone in *The Paradise Papers*[17] throws light on an older and deeper transition. As a potter she became interested in the goddess figurines from grave sites, some up to 25,000 years old. In this pre-history women were credited with magical powers for their ability to produce babies. At some point the role of the male in procreation was realised with the penis as the magic wand. *The Paradise Papers* charts the 7,000 year story, set in the Middle East, of the overcoming of matrilineal cultures by patriarchal societies. One of the last enclaves was in the Arabian Peninsula. Mecca was once a great pagan goddess-worshipping temple. It was this culture that Mohammed and his followers set out to overthrow.

It won't take 7,000 years this time! The new economic and informational reality of the de facto power of the young is coming up against traditional power relations in which the old have held the levers of power: economic, political, judicial, military. This is relevant to our struggle as values warriors to work for the future of planet Earth.

THE REVOLT OF THE YOUNG

A case has been argued above that, in the so called first world, the combination of twelvefold over-consumption and maybe 25% excess longevity[18] should be the central focus for values warriors – campaigners for planet centred values – in the coming decades.

Now throughout history countless idealist thinkers, writers and movements, both religious and secular, have presented their cases for what they saw as 'the world as it should be'. What they failed to demonstrate was the *engine of change*. Without this they were forced to fall back on argument and exhortation: "can't you see that this would lead to a better world?"

(This charge can certainly not be levelled against Marxists. Marx and Engels thought that they had identified the motor of change in the inevitable struggle of the proletariat for emancipation. The fact that 'the revolution' appears to have failed can be put down to their ideology not understanding human psychology as well as it understood economics – pithily demonstrated by George Orwell in *Animal Farm*[19].)

How does this lack of agency relate to the struggle for planet centred values? Organisations such as Population Matters[20] are committed to drawing attention to the population issue and the consequences of not facing up to this. Its membership and supporters are mainly (not exclusively) 'mature' and in general comfortably off. They are for the most part well beyond child-begetting age themselves. Unsurprising then that their focus is on lower procreation rates in the third world with some argument for child benefit limitations for larger families here and moral encouragement to families still of child producing age to "stop at two".

XIII. Energy of Youth

For just as (with honourable exceptions) the rich and powerful will never voluntarily give up their influence in society so (again with honourable exceptions) the old are unlikely to voluntarily surrender their 'place in the sun' – not even for the sake of future life on this planet.

Before taking this argument forward, some rough definitions. The threshold of maturity (euphemism for age) has already been taken as 'three score years and ten' i.e. seventy years. 'The young', in this context are defined more broadly than 'youth' in common usage: maybe up to fifty years. The point is that these and their growing children will bear the brunt of the backlash – of 'Gaia's Revenge'[21] – as the repercussions of generations of human arrogance and wilful ignorance are visited back on all life.

Within these definitions the revolt of the young has, in this opinion, the potential to transform 'the relations of production'. To be the engine of change. They have both the incentive and the tools.

The question for those of us who are *not* young – yet believe we care for this planet, for the biosphere, for a viable future … is where we will choose to stand in the coming period of transition between the catastrophe that exists now and a future that offers some hope.

Are we on board for the journey?

MAKING A START

The earlier discussion ["Exit Is Not Easy"] highlighted the difficulties, both practical and cultural, for anyone considering an exit decision for positive reasons. This is now revisited in the context of the cultural revolution that the young may bring about.

Making room sums up the need. It is both the central notion and a rallying cry.

There are already two groups of 'mature' people ready and willing to respond to the need of the age *if* social permissions are in place.

The first group, already defined as values warriors, are motivated to defend the biosphere, to literally make room for life: including their own offspring (grandchildren and beyond); including *your* offspring; including all the life forms and ecosystems of the planet.

The second group spans many people who may not be terminally ill, nor are they suicidal, but who are no longer hungry for life: they are simply ready to leave – or would be if positive social permission existed. They would be happy to make room.

Instead, the message from many societies today is: "thou shalt not die – we will decide for you". The glaring contradiction is that it is considered acceptable and honourable to die for your country (meaning the state that claims you) – indeed you may be conscripted to do so – yet not acceptable to choose to make room on the planet for the best of social and ecological reasons. (This is where Exit International[16] – a worldwide network – deserves credit for being non-judgemental. Their aim is to provide up to date information on both legal and practical issues.)

Although the final need will be securing legal changes in those regimes still resistant to granting the ultimate democratic right, the vital stage before that is winning the cultural argument and gaining social permission. Or rather, two arguments requiring two campaigns.

First, an attitude shift that positive exit by someone of sound mind should not be classed as suicide. (It is notable that coroner's verdicts frequently record: "suicide while the balance of the mind was disturbed".)

Second, a campaign for the right of any person, including medical professionals, to be free from the fear of prosecution for assisting exit where written proof of intention exists and other safeguards are in place. This protection already exists in many jurisdictions.

Good people, including but not limited to ecocentric campaigners, can play their part for the future of all life by giving their support to these cultural struggles.

Albert Einstein is reported to have said "It is tasteless to prolong life artificially. [When] it is time to go i will do it elegantly."

XIV. *Albert Einstein*

BRINGING IT ALL TOGETHER

It may appear that this essay embraces several disjointed themes. The threads are woven around three core notions: -

Enchantment:
being enchanted; defending enchantment.

Understanding:
tools for understanding that span both sides of life.

Courage:
moral and physical courage.

Our world, our universe no less, is amazing. Its enchantment can take our breath away – but not in a nice, sanitised, pretty sense. Pain and loss and death and the predator taking its prey are as much a part of the rich tapestry as joy and awe and discovery and revelling in powers and quiet fulfilment. No one grasped this better than Nietzsche.

So how would we not want to defend an enchanted world against all that reduces it to mere resources, to instruments, to assets on a balance sheet?

To act one needs to understand. Obvious. So this understanding now needs to be comprehensive – to take in both aspects of the world. The cleverness of the enlightenment is no longer enough: was never enough.

The bringing back together of science and spirit can create a wisdom worthy of the challenges we face. In the field of social theory and practice, of social structure and passion, we do have tools that can guide us if we have the courage to follow where the wisdom leads...

Physical courage is about immediate situations. None of us can know how we will stand up until the moment arrives. Nothing more to say.

Moral courage is an ongoing challenge. Facing up to realities that we would rather not confront, whether about ourselves or the world, can be incredibly hard.

In the extreme case it gives rise to the phenomenon that psycho-analysts study as repression into the unconscious of thoughts and feelings that we do not want to own. More commonly, we can choose to be in denial – both as individuals and as social groups – about physical and social realities that should challenge us to act.

For values warriors this is a double challenge: both confronting denial in ourselves and accepting that the attitudes of those around us may not be simply due to lack of information/education.

Can we encourage each other to be brave, to argue for unpalatable responses for the sake of all life? Perhaps to be despised?

Woody Wood

October 2017

A JOURNEY – Appendix A

STATISTICS ON POPULATION CONSUMPTION AND LONGEVITY

World human population today .... 7.4 Billion people.

Of these, 'First World' (approx.) .... 1.0 Billion people.

So rest of World ....6.4 Billion people.

[Source: Worldometers : World population clock]

Consumption measured by per capita income (all figures in dollars):

First World income $10,000

'Developing' World $850

So ratio = 10/.85 = 12

[Source: Physics fact book/money/income of average person]

First World longevity from birth = 81 years   *[Source: Wikipedia]*

But this includes childhood deaths etc.

Estimated adult first world longevity = 88 years

[Various sources: this figure can be debated, dependent on the starting point taken]

So total lifespan First World consumption = $10,000 x 88 = $880,000

Now **if** First World lifespans were limited to three score years and ten = 70 years

Then lifetime consumption in First World would be reduced by 70/88

= a factor of 0.8 approx.

For simplicity take impact on Planet Earth of human activity to be population times consumption (ignoring technology)

So, $I = P \times C$

For reference take 'developing' World per capita consumption as one unit

i.e. $C_{dw} = 1$

So, impact on planet:

$I_{dw} = C_{dw} \times P_{dw} = 1 \times 6.4$ Billion = 6.4 Billlion units.

Now First World per capita consumption $C_{fw} = 12$ units

So, First World impact = $I_{fw} = C_{fw} \times P_{fw} = 12 \times 1 = 12$ Billion units

So, one Billion First World people have almost twice the impact on the Planet as 6.4 Billion 'Developing' World people!

Thus total impact at present = 18.4 Billion units!!

This puts 'developing' World population in perspective:
only one third of the problem!

If First World lifespans were limited to 70 years (still way beyond 'developing' World lifespans) then First World impact would be reduced by a factor of 0.8

$I_{fw} = C_{fw} \times P_{fw} \times F = 12 \times 1$ Billion $\times 0.8 = 9.6$ Billion units.

So, total population impact on the Planet would be:

6.4 bn units + 9.6 bn units = 16 Billion units

This is a significant reduction on present impact of 18.4 billion units and this would not be accompanied by further effects of an ageing population.

A JOURNEY – Appendix B

LOCALISM AND REGIONALISM

LOCALISM AND REGIONALISM

With the gradual yielding of a collective to an individualist social ethos; with the hollowing out of local government power; with the weakening of trade union influence; with the decline of local and community newspapers … both individuals and nuclear families feel powerless before the Westminster run state. (As every devolutionist knows, England, Scotland, Wales(Cymru) and Kernow are historic nations whereas 'Britain' is properly understood as the rump of an empire.)

Meanwhile, modern states feel constrained before the imperatives of the Neoliberal market. We are told that there is no alternative to 'growing the economy' – even though local jobs continue to be lost and goods once produced locally are imported over great distances.

In principle, regional and local societies and economies at least partially protected from the Neoliberal hypermarket economy would be more stable, as philosopher John Gray has argued[22]. They could also be more sustainable in the longer term. In particular, their ability to prioritise ecological policies could give our planet a chance of recovery in conjunction with other actions.

It is argued now that these local and regional objectives of *progressive protectionism*[23] should form part of our deep green strategy.

Unfortunately there are presently two major obstacles to be overcome before viable local and regional communities with their appropriate levels of economic activity could become serious prospects.

UNSUSTAINABLE CONSUMPTION

The first of these is that most people, most families, are wedded to levels of consumption that the planet-stripping global economy presently provides for us. The fact that this will not last is cold comfort since at that point the descent into chaos will likely make any constructive social projects impossible.

Thus some of our social energy must needs be focused on transition strategies towards lower material consumption, combined with maintained or enhanced quality of life – a soft landing if you like.

Such strategies might include: -

➢ Expectation lowering via peer group influence and 'permission'.

➢ Expense avoidance from resource sharing and collective purchasing.

➢ Savings from off grid energy schemes etc.

➢ Locally created main jobs, where possible.

➢ Supplementary incomes from 'side' projects.

➢ Local currencies to facilitate the above.

➢ Low level sharing via bread funds etc.

➢ Local revenue for local services from subscribed bonds rather than from taxation.

FRAGILE COMMUNITIES

The second obstacle to effective local and regional societies and economies is the bigger challenge: fragmentation of our community strengths leading to a sense of powerlessness and alienation as mentioned at the beginning.

Responding to this requires some understanding of social structure and social dynamics: how societies hang together.

The key point to grasp is that all communities and societies, both human and animal, do have structure. They are not just collections of individuals. Some aspects of social structure were explored in the Social Story of *Values for Our Time*[24].

Much critical discussion about society in general is focussed on power: who has it, who should have it and how they might be held to account by the rest of society. Talking of power, an important distinction needs to be made between dominating power, power over, and enabling power. In this second positive sense the trait is better defined as avoidance of powerlessness. In a social context it can provide natural community leaders.

The usually missing story is about responsibility: who is up for it, who seeks to avoid it and how they/we compensate for that as natural followers. (These roles can change or reverse but that is going a bit deep for this purpose.)

This complementary relationship – in *Devolve!* language between leaderful Divergents and followful Convergents – forms the bedrock of all social groups.

A further aspect of social communities links scale, size, to diversity and speciality: the sub-group. In the words of D.W. Harding[25]: "Group psychology … is sub-group psychology." Through our sub-groups we are able to follow our interests and concerns, enjoy comradeship, find roles that suit us … while at the same time enriching the fabric of society as a whole.

Many local sub-groups form chains or networks across societies that can aspire to social influence. Examples include the Women's Institute, the RSPB and of course trade unions. Yet their foundations lie in their local groups or branches.

Clearly this phenomenon is critical to our search for viable local and regional societies.

WHY THE FAILURE?

So why are our local communities so disempowered? Why are individuals so disengaged? Three reasons are suggested here, though there may be others.

First, the auto re-enforcing effect of an age and culture of individualism. Where there are fewer viable local associations and democratic positions in which leaderful humans can find roles, such people will direct their energies to personal advancement in the wider society – and devil take the hindmost.

Second, central states and authorities are instinctively hostile to what they perceive as rival centres of power, even potential ones. Divide and rule is the precautionary principle. The [anti]combination acts passed by Westminster parliaments in the early years of trade unions were classic examples. More recently the undermining of local education authorities by state authorised academies is but one example of the incremental dis-empowerment of local government.

Third, we can note the taking over of people's minds by central and global media. The point of reference on many issues may now be TV programmes (in which people are passive) rather than face to face local groups (in which we can be active participants). In passing it may be noted that here there can be an unholy alliance between elements of The System and responsibility avoiding, followful Convergents. In this sense mass media can be said to have hijacked local community just as the central state has hijacked regional and national identities. [For English regionalists it remains a bitter pill that Wessex (say) and English identities are being marginalised by a state sponsored British identity. The Brexit tensions have many levels but at one level they reflect the revolt of a historic bonded Englishness against a cosmopolitan Britishness that plays into the Neoliberal agenda.]

MORE CHALLENGES

Drawing these strands together, we can summarise the mountains we have to climb: the transition to more modest yet more realistic local incomes and economies; the re-energising of participatory local communities using the tools of social wisdom available to us.

The first challenge has already been examined above. So it is the second task – supporting the revival of vibrant and diverse local associations within our communities – that needs to demand our attention.

Some strategies to be discussed: -

➢ As activists who care for our communities (and the planet) giving a chunk of our own time to this – making a commitment.

➢ Recognising, supporting, sometimes joining sub-groups: community of interest associations and groups of all types.

➢ Participating in or supporting activities of such groups: bring and buy days; charity runs; text discussions.

➢ Supporting leaderful Divergents within groups; not seeing them as threats or automatically as ego trippers.

➢ Trying to decide when and where to engage directly with existing local politics and when rather to form or support independent platforms around social issues.

➢ Attempting to co-ordinate local voting pacts on relevant issues.

➢ Supporting where appropriate local/regional direct action campaigns. Paying attention to the use and control of land.

➢ Taking full advantage of old and new legal co-operative structures.

➢ Promoting local and regional pride and identity plus a revival of local media in support of this aim.

➢ Setting up local sub-nets alongside the internet: linking these to positive social media and engagement with the young.

A JOURNEY – Appendix C

ASSUMPTIONS AND VALUES

Wherever and whenever humans (like other social animals) have to live in association with one another they (we) have needed to share a great number of assumptions about what the other will/will not do. (Even at the most basic level it may be an assumption held in common that one does not push into the queue!) Thus members of any viable and continuing group have needed to hold values in common.

In this sense the notion of assumptions and the concept of values are virtually interchangeable. Friedrich Nietzsche: "Every people sets up a table of values over themselves."

Notice the word 'people'. In historic social groups back into pre-human times it was virtually impossible for an individual to survive alone. Only with the emergence of surplus value (see main essay, page 24) in more complex and structured societies did partial autonomy allow (some) individuals to have identities that were more than mere personalities. Nietzsche again: "The human individual is a recent invention".

To be clear: our inter-dependence is still very real but it is now at arms-length and can be invisible, giving the illusion (and the self-illusion) of ourselves as autonomous individuals able to claim 'rights' – especially if social rules have emerged allowing most of us to claim a share of common wealth as personal property: even if only as wages.

CONFLICTING ASSUMPTIONS

The potential for conflicting assumptions has always existed.

Historically these tensions could be divided into two classes. First, geographical conflicts *between* tribes/cultures (whether boundary disputes or subsistence tensions (say between pastoral cultures needing open grazing for cattle and agricultural cultures needing fenced land for growing their crops). Second, temporal struggles between older and newer practices and values *within* cultures: sometimes inter-generational.

With the emergence of empires including and incorporating several tribes or peoples under an imperial law, a new and scary conflict of assumptions became visible. This was an early example of the 'absolute versus relative' tension which has vexed philosophers, bedevilled political discourse and arguably shed more blood than any other clash of assumptions in history.

On the one hand there is a master assumption of universal values, growing out of the 'might is right' law making of empires, sanctified by the 'one objective truth' assumption of the enlightenment and emblazoned on the banners of liberal individualism. Following from this the two consequent assumptions are:

"There are universal values and we know what they are."

and:

"We need to challenge and stamp out 'wrong' values and beliefs."

Think you don't fall into this trap? Where do you stand on cliterodectomy?

On the other hand stands the fundamental assumption that all values are relative: originally the 'table of values' relative to the tribe or culture. The consequent assumptions that can follow from this are:

"Our values are right for us as a people and we have the 'right' to defend them."

"Respect for other cultures/value systems."

"Challenges to dominant yet questionable values need to come from *within* the culture."

"Showing humility in this modern age. Since we cannot be 'absolutely' right we might just be wrong after all."

Some of the most perceptive thinkers have understood the tragic quality of the absolute – relative dilemma and in some cases argued the relative case. These include Machiavelli, Nietzsche, Isiah Berlin and John Gray.

ASSUMPTIONS AND ECOCENTRISM

Those of us who take an ecocentric or planet centred approach – who define ourselves as values warriors for our planet and its ecosystems – have first to recognise that the assumption that the planet must come first is just another assumption, no matter how much 'evidence' we bring to bear.

With this caution in mind we can state clearly and forcefully our core assumption:

"That the fate of the whole network of interlocking ecosystems on planet Earth is (should be) our primary concern."

and the implied assumption:

"That human concerns need to be placed in this broader context."

Within this overall stance there is scope for disagreements among those sharing an ecocentric standpoint.

These disagreements over further assumptions perhaps fall into four classes:

➤ The weightings to be given to the various destructive factors.

➤ The causes or sources of these threats to our planet.

➤ The responses or actions needed.

➤ The red lines that should not be crossed.

Some examples of threats that can be taken as more or less critical: climate change; pollution of the oceans; habitat destruction.

The primary causes of these threats: social/political structures (blame the baddies); bad/dangerous technology (techno-fix); excess human consumption by some groups (see main essay); world population (see main essay) (a) Birth rate too high; (b) Death rate too low; some combination of all these factors.

The response choices. For many ecocentric warriors the primary assumption is a general lack of awareness/ understanding among people at large – calling for an educational/outreaching response. Such allies have this stance in common with all believers, from Marxists to evangelical faith groups. (e.g. Marxists talk about false consciousness.)

An alternative assumption is that most people are aware in general terms of the threatened future yet have other reasons for not responding as activists would wish. These can range from sheer lack of emotional energy to go beyond coping with daily life, through a fatalist acceptance of an inevitable (and perhaps deserved!) future … to the classic convergent response that "someone else should lead on this". One implication of this assumption is that self-styled values warriors should indeed lead (see below).

This leads on to the next pair of alternative assumptions. On the one hand that only governments can act effectively on the required scale, with the implication that intense lobbying of governments is the way forward. (As argued in the main essay, this approach can be blind to the relative impotence of governments, constrained by many lobbies: big business, media, establishment interests, even electors!)

Other values warriors make the assumption, hold the conviction, that action by people in their real situations has to be the starting point. Yet this conviction leads to a further range of assumptions (not always mutually exclusive).

At one end that action must come from *other* people, from certain groups of people: for example women in Africa. This implies a follow-on assumption that these groups need to be encouraged, assisted, enabled to change life decisions and social outcomes.

At the other end of this spectrum is the conviction that action in defence of our biosphere must start with *ourselves*: for integrity; for example; for inspiration.

Finally there can be disagreement over red lines: over the extent to which the end *does not* always justify the means.

These can include: eugenicist strategies; socially coercive strategies; challenges to human social justice agendas; challenges to personal liberty standpoints.

THE ASSUMPTION TRAIL

It should now be clear that "save the planet" – a great mantra – is not as straightforward as it seems.

Now one thing that comes out of the above exploration is the concept of an *assumption trail*: a sequence of options that both groups and individual eco warriors may choose (or feel obliged) to make.

At this point i should perhaps nail my own colours to the mast, holding (at this time: our assumptions may change as the world acts on us) a radical minority position even among values warriors.

I share of course the core assumption that the fate of earth's ecosystems should be our primary concern: they 'need' to be viable long after we are gone. Also the follow on assumption that human concerns should not take precedence over this goal.

On the issue of the primary threat, my conviction is that species destruction due to habitat loss is the most serious aspect of human induced damage.

As to main causes, for me a combination of world population and First World excess consumption is a toxic mix. Within this context i part company with many allies in recognising the low death rate in affluent cultures due to extended longevity as both a great contributor to accelerating eco-destruction and a personal challenge.

In terms of how we should respond i share with many others grave doubts over the widely held assumption that most people need to be informed/educated about the situation. The Convergence – Divergence theory developed by *Devolve!* lends support to the alternative assumption that lack of motivation among the majority is not down to lack of information or understanding.

With regard to strategy i have long argued against the Fabian fallacy that "only governments can sort it". My own assumption is that any human response needs to be people led.

But which people? The assumption that this should primarily be "other people" seems to me to be dubious on both strategic and integrity grounds. My conviction is that action has to start with ourselves as values warriors.

When it comes to red lines eugenics has to be beyond the pale for me. It conflicts with the core principle of an enchanted approach to the world: humility – not trying to play god with nature.

There is a similar, though more pragmatic, objection to coercion strategies on my part. One question is: who does the coercing? The situation would need to be so dire to cross this red line that social structures would likely be in collapse mode already.

Very different response from me to the social justice campaign. For a start it betrays a very human centred approach: what about justice for other creatures? Beyond this many of the campaigners for social justice for deprived human groups are in wilful denial over ecocentric issues such as population density.

Personal liberty? The previous critique of liberal individualism as one of the components of modern alienation answers this question. The valid aspects of concern for personal liberty are better covered under the heading of social liberty. In other dimensions 'personal liberty' is strictly a code name for personal licence – usually an option only for those who have the means to exercise it. So no red line here.

A JOURNEY – Appendix D

THE LONGEVITY QUESTION

THE LONGEVITY QUESTION

One of the themes of this essay has been that in facing up to human impacts on our planet we need to take a broad view. Alongside the population issue the impacts of first world consumption and first world longevity need to be responded to. (N.B. longevity = consumption x time.)

The values of the dominant culture today are strongly homocentric ("Us first, us first at all costs"). As the essay has argued this includes seeing the preservation and extension of human life and the conquest of death as both a value and a goal.

Challenging these values on behalf of our fellow creatures and the biosphere ('Gaia') has been seen as a challenge for humans (meaning those of us who have become planet centred).

As is so often the case, nature got there first.

The diagram and text reproduced as Plate XV is an extract from a scientific paper (see credits and references[26]) demonstrating that in all creatures including humans natural defences to ageing processes – such as anti-oxidant defences – are programmed to weaken after the most productive phase of life (in humans reproduction and child rearing).

This 'report from nature' confirms what some of us instinctively knew: that the enormous scientific and medical resources (a major component of modern first world consumption) being devoted to extending the lives of some humans are un-natural in the deepest sense.

Such activity – and the ideology that drives it – constitutes a threat to the entire web of life, to our own children (who will be picking up the pieces if they can) and to the age balance of existing society.

As already noted in this essay, we values warriors have the very unpopular task of bringing these consequences into focus just as so many other fractures and conflicts darken the skies for the World as viewed from a human-centred standpoint. In the words of a former government chief scientific officer: "a perfect storm in thirty years".

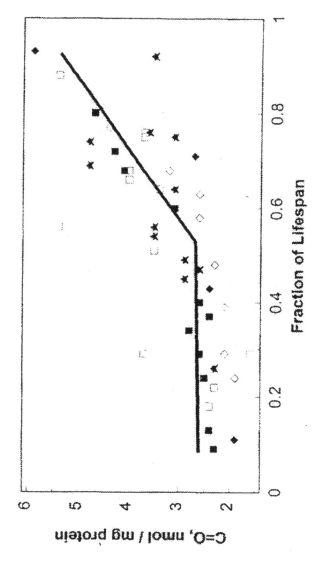

Fig. 1. Carbonyl content of protein from different tissues. One observes a dramatic increase in oxidized protein during the last third of the lifespan. The line is the semi-logarithmic fit to all the data points. The data points were taken from published reports: ■, human dermal fibroblasts in tissue culture (Oliver et al., 1987); ★, human lens (Garland, 1990); ☐, human brain obtained at autopsy (Smith et al., 1991); ◆, rat liver (Starke-Reed and Oliver, 1989); and ◇, whole fly (Sohal et al., 1993).

oxidatively modified proteins observed during aging will have serious deleterious effects on cellular and organ function.

XV. Programmed to Die

A JOURNEY – Appendix E

PLANET CENTRED
FORUM

MISSION STATEMENT

The human species is causing devastation to a planet that it shares with a vast, but declining, number of other life forms. There is an ethical imperative to modify our impact as a species to a level that is compatible with the continued vitality of the planet's interlinked ecosystems and that permits their recovery. This can be done by rejecting an anthropocentric viewpoint in favour of a web-of-life perspective: humans are part of this web of life, not separate from it, and so if immediate human interests clash with ecosystem interests the latter must be given priority.

The specific aims of this forum are to promote the study and critical analysis of relevant issues and to provide practical support to each other, and to others, in striving to live reduced-impact lives. Further, to promote planet centred thinking on issues such as human overpopulation, overconsumption and planet threatening technologies.

A JOURNEY

REFERENCES

REFERENCES (A: TO MAIN ESSAY)

1. *Values for Our Time* Published *Devolve!* 2014 paperback   ISBN 978 0993112607 also *Which Values? Devolve!* 2015 paperback
ISBN 978 0993112614

2. *On The Origin of The Species* Charles Darwin Oxford University Press 2008 paperback
ISBN 978 0199219223

3. For example *The Selfish Gene* Richard Dawkins OUP 2006 paperback edition
ISBN 978 0199201151

4. *A New Science of Life* Rupert Sheldrake Icon Books 2009 paperback edition
ISBN 978 1848310421

5. *The Origin of Consciousness in The Breakdown of The Bicameral Mind* Julian Jaynes   Mariner Books 2000 paperback edition
ISBN 978 0618057072

6. Planet Centred Forum   Ecocentric Network   Mission Statement at Appendix E

7. See reference 1 above. Social Story (chapter) from Page 25

8. *The Alienation of Modern Man*   Fritz Pappenheim
    Monthly Review Press 1968 paperback edition
    SBN 853450056

9. See for example page 38 in *Ecological Ethics* Patrick
    Curry Polity Press 2011 paperback edition
    ISBN 978 0745651262

10. Explore many aspects of enchantment in *Deep Roots in
    A Time of Frost – Essays on Tolkien* Patrick Curry
    Walking Tree Books 2014 paperback
    ISBN 978 3905703337

11. See reference 1 above. Values Warriors defined as
    advocates and defenders of planet centred values.

12. *An Essay on The Principle of Population*   T.R. Malthus
    Oxford University Press 2008 reprint of 1798 edition
    ISBN 978 0199540457

13. *The Ecology of Freedom* Murray Bookchin Cheshire
    Books Inc. 1982 paperback edition
    ISBN 0917352106

14. E.g. Ian Whyte, convenor Ecocentric Alliance (Canada)
    Essay to be published.

15. Dignity in Dying 0207 479 7730
    www.dignityindying.org.uk

16. Exit International 02071931557 Exitinternational.net

17. *The Paradise Papers* Merlin Stone Illustrated edition
    Published by Virago Limited 1977 ISBN 0704338076

18. Refer to Appendix A.

19. *Animal Farm* George Orwell Penguin 2008 paperback
    ISBN 978 0141036137

20. Population Matters (formerly known as Optimum
    Population Trust). www.populationmatters.org

21. *The Revenge of Gaia* James Lovelock Penguin 2007
    paperback edition
    ISBN 0141025972

REFERENCES (B: TO APPENDIX B)

22. John Gray, author of *Enlightenment's Wake* and other
    books, in an interview in *The Big Issue* N° 863,
    September 7-13 2009.

23. Concept argued for by Colin Hines, author of
    Localisation: A Global Manifesto published 2000 by
    Earthscan
    ISBN 978 1853836121 *Progressive Protectionism* now
    published as an e-book.

24. See reference 1 above: the Social Story of *Values for Our Time.*

25. *Social Psychology and Individual Values* D.W. Harding
    Hutchinson University Library 1966 edition
    ISBN 978 0090426324

REFERENCES (C: to appendix D)

26. *Experimental Gerontology* ISSN 0531-5565 Volume 36,
    Issue 9 (Sep 2001) pages 1495-1502: Oxidative
    modification of proteins during ageing. Rodney L Levine
    and Earl R Stadtman.